MW01233853

MORPH

jessie carty

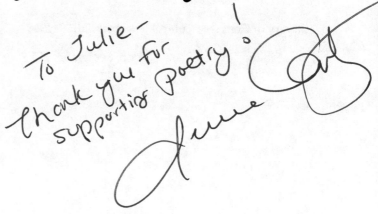

*To Julie —
Thank you for
supporting poetry!*

Alexander, Arkansas
www.SiblingRivalryPress.com

Morph
Copyright © 2013 by Jessie Carty

Cover design by Mona Z. Kraculdy

Cover art by Ellaraine Lockie

Sibling Rivalry Press, LLC
13913 Magnolia Glen Drive
Alexander, AR 72002

www.siblingrivalrypress.com
info@siblingrivalrypress.com

ISBN: 978-1-937420-49-9

Library of Congress Control Number: 2013941988

First Sibling Rivalry Press Edition, September 2013

In Memory of My Father
Richard Dahls Arnesen, Sr.
(1945–2012)

X

Y

Z

MORPH

AMPHIBIOGENESIS IN TWO VOICES
with J. S. G.

1.

The way your skin
folds at your joints
reminds me of an infant.
But even though you are young
in frog years, you are not
a newborn because if
you were new you'd be
aquatic, just head and tail and gills
wriggling free of a jellied egg
not un-like cartoon
representations of sperm
in reverse. No, you would not
be yet here, poised
amidst rocks absorbing air
through skin and lungs.

2.

What if we could morph?
If. Instead of articulate
speech and bipedal form,
we could go from child
to a second life of wings,
formed from limb-buds
tucked under our shoulder blades,
our bodies no longer haired
but feathered as we soar
within a liquid sky
so nothing remains vestigial.

AT 13

Every year at the end of May, the city blocks off River Road with white sawhorses between Water Street and the bypass for Highway 17. Riverspree.

This is the year I get to go by myself. I'm early.

Over on the big bandstand someone is sound-checking a bluegrass guitar.

To my right, little girls practice flying in homemade wings above a concrete slab that will soon be a recital stage.

For lunch, I buy a cheese and chicken divan filled with grilled onions and wrapped up in greasy foil. Its peppered juices sting the skin of my chin.

The rest of my money is burning a hole in my pocket. Maybe I need a shirt airbrushed with my name in pink? Or perhaps my own bottled beach of neon sand?

It's dark now and everyone is watching the fireworks shouting yellow and blue.

I feel itchy in my new unicorn shirt that is two sizes too big.

Tomorrow I will peel like dried glue, revealing new, red skin.

EVERYONE NAMED HER BRIGHT
after Rachel Aviv's article "Like I was Jesus"

which she thought meant she glowed.
She did not connect her ability to read
with an intellectual brilliance.
She wanted to actually see
herself shining like that moment before
the light went out in the refrigerator.

Everyone named her bright.

In those same early years,
before school, she pictured Jesus
as a flower, curling up from his
grave because he rose. She didn't
understand how he could be
so beautiful and also so constantly
cross until she thought

(everyone named her bright)

of how easily she could move
from playtime to anger by finding
yet another hole in the white dress
she favored for her favorite doll. The doll
which she often left naked on the edge
of the tub as she waited for it to be altered.

Everyone named her bright.

FIELD TRIP

It was a two hour drive from my school to the Norfolk Zoo.
On the bus ride, I hovered around the chaperoning mothers,

especially Mrs. Harvey. I loved that on top of her little round
head, her hair sat in a small afro

that reminded me of a gumdrop. She sang "Jesse's Girl" to me
while she and the other mothers talked about how

fine the singer was. I wanted to like the song
but in it, Jesse is a boy. Except for me, Jesse

is always a boy. At the zoo, I stuck close to Mrs. Harvey
until we arrived at the Nocturnal Habitat. She didn't

want to see no rodents. Inside I tried to follow my teacher's
shirt while I kept my hand on the left wall as my class

passed through the rooms of raccoons, shrews, and possums.
The girls huddled, whispering about the boys

who were lined up in front of the enclosures, tapping
on the glass. There was just enough space for one

more. With my hand below the glass, I placed my face
against the window. There was one

bat hanging from a branch near my corner. I
was the only one who saw his beady eye.

LITTLE BORDERS

I'm trying to pinpoint
my first memory of you.

You aren't there
when I'm getting dressed

for school. You aren't
where I wait for the bus

or at the Christmas
pageant. Instead

you are on the couch
in indeterminate

years, saying too loudly—
again, again, again—

because you decided
to quiz me

on my spelling words
until I had a headache;

until I began spelling
everything wrong; until

I'm also on the couch
after crying. I'm

perched on your hip.
You are laying

on your left side
and so am I. My

left hip to your
right. We are

planks of wood
or countries

with ever-changing
borders because

of little wars, tiny
battles, moments

of appeasement.
When you sit up

I roll off. I
begin to scratch

your back
—hard—

just like
you like.

NEW KID

He dared to choose her as his protector
on the first day of class because,

while she wore a bow in her hair, her
knuckles were rough like stripped

metal. He didn't choose an enemy
straight off. He just kept an eye

out for whomever kept their distance,
yet couldn't stop looking at him.

He knew that person (or them)
would eventually give him

a nickname. Not the good kind
like Bro or maybe Junior. No,

they'd go for it. They'd pick
on his hair, his clothes,

anything just a bit off
from what they

deemed to be
the center

of this school's
universe.

THE BOY WHO'D NEVER SEEN SNOW

God, I was in love with you.
After four hours

on your first day,
I had named our children.

All I knew was your name,
and that you had moved

from Florida.
Exotic.

And bless you. You
were short like me.

By the second month,
I'd pictured

slow dancing with you
in the gym.

Then it snowed.
I watched you

stare out the classroom window
while we waited

for the early dismissal buses.
There was a light

dusting, enough to close
an inter-coastal school.

This small amount
was your first.

We shared that
from across the classroom

like a first kiss. A kiss
cold enough

to raise the hairs
on my arms.

SHORT GIRL AT THE THEME PARK

She was my first
roller coaster:
The Loch Ness Monster.
I was eight and too small
to ride the big swing
but tall enough
for a double looping
creature of black
and yellow metal.
My uncle rode with me
and I can still hear
his screams, still feel
the mechanical clack
of the track as we climbed.
From the front car,
we stared, suspended
for what seemed hours
before we hurtled
into the first dive. I
loved the weightlessness
of my feet and the weight
of my chest against
the harness. I laughed
as we slid around
the curves of the beast.

WHAT I THOUGHT AFTER FABIO WAS HIT
IN THE FACE BY A BIRD AT BUSCH GARDENS

I was never interested in romance novels. I wanted to be
excited by women clinging on muscular men, but I

instead pined for suits of armor, elven women
who worked magic and fantasies that did not involve

engagements rings. Although fantasy novels aren't always
kind to women, they still seem more real

than mechanics who behave like princes or
soccer stars who fall for the four-eyed

chubby girl from math class. No, those guys seem unreal.
A water nymph, a dragon, a spot of magic, however,

is something I at least can imagine.

WHAT WOULD BUFFY DO?

She wasn't the first
to be the slayer
but she always
felt like the last.

Who knew I
would relate to
a blonde former
cheerleader who

hunted vampires?
Perhaps it was her
reluctant acceptance
of her destiny, of

her power, of her
eventual embrace
of everything she
was supposed

to destroy or was it
how the dark needed
her? That she spent
seven seasons, spanned

two networks, one
virtually unrelated
movie kicking past
commercial breaks

and coming-soon
trailers to save
the world, one
hour at a time.

ZOMBIE GIRL'S LAMENT

Everyone whispers the word when I walk away—
braaaaaaains—a long drawn out syllable

But—for me—it isn't about brains
What I hear—like a round inside my skull

is—*wet want*—and a need for something
smooth—silky

I understand vampires and their need
for the tang of metal in blood

and maybe I *would* want brains
if I lived in a world without

ice cream—yogurt—or microwaved
Twinkies melting into mush

LEARNING TO COUNT

Digits scare me. The way
they crease and crack. Their

squarish yet curved shapes
that defy category. They are

your first attempt at counting
as well as your first declaration

of I as you point back
to yourself. *I want. I stomp. I*

fear. But, we quickly move from
1 to the full 10 count of desires

or terrors so that we have to
create numbers beyond what

we can see or grasp. For fingers
can be cupped, can hold

all the unseen bits that fill
what we call empty space.

DIAGRAMMING SENTENCES

Childhood is a noun. It is this tiny person I was. It is a place of self-imposed structure where my siblings and I made rules about who would get to watch what on our wood-paneled console TV. From three channels we'd each get half an hour, or if we wanted an hour-long show, we had to forfeit a turn. The order was set up by whoever got out of bed first, therefore, I never slept in. Childhood is a thing like a cabinet: closed but accessible. Childhood is an idea. It is: I wandered lonely as a cloud. Childhood could be a verb. It could be active, predicated. It is what we hear with our inside voices.

DRAWN TO HEROES

Mom always purchased the leftover comics
at the end of the month from Woodard's Drug.

I was in love with too many of them
to pick a favorite. I'd read anything.

I wanted to look like Dazzler with her blonde hair
and roller skates or

at least I thought I could be Betty with her tomboyish charm.
I was drawn to the scrappy

heroes like the unsung Power Pack while my brother
championed the usual Spider Men and Batboys

as if he hoped he'd wake one day
having been bitten

by a radioactive moth or to have suddenly discovered
he was actually adopted

and that his real parents left him all their wealth
along with

a hermit crab shell the size of Manhattan
that could be his fortress

because we thought everything large
was the size of Manhattan.

DRAGON

(S)he's the light
of the stage, a yellow
bo(a) around the thighs,
artfully tucked, one end
in (t)his hand makes a roar
like a drag(on) queen
protecting a throbbing
(egg) ready to birth.

THE EGG DREAM

Oval. Oblong. Stretch into a pumpkin. Orange. Pie. Three
slices. A prime number. Prime rib. Adam's offering. Did he get
it back? It doesn't say. It should be important to know if the
sons of Adam are flawed. They are Number One. And I have
two instead of one. Ovaries. Not one lone horn like a unicorn.
The circus claimed it was not a fake. See, the rider trying to
move the horn to show it was intact. It didn't come off. It only
wiggled. A goat with a mutation. One instead of two. Times
two because the point must be made to equal four. And there
are four cards in a game of War. Four. With two decks of cards
a game could last for hours. A red deck. A blue deck. If I
remember coloring you were always blue. Even in pastels.
When dyeing eggs. Easter eggs without church. Eggs hidden
in the backyard as if they would grow.

FUNCTION OF X

We grew up east
of everything. We
reckoned no one knew
our names, our town
our composures.
We died daily
of hyperbole
because of course
there are
smaller cities,
tinier streets.

We wanted to be
all of the army
where $f(x) = x^2$,
where an input of 2
meant we were
four, or function
of imaginary friends
who wrote
of our adventures
like an equation
that easily solved

a summer without
camps or family
vacations. We
could solve the "What
You Did Last Summer"
essay by using
our fact. Which
was everyone else's
definition of fiction.

FOREST

I look down at the page, but instead of forest I read, "for rest."
And isn't that what a wooded yard is good for?

Good as a place to hang up a hammock; as an area in which
to hug a tree as you try to climb up, up and away.

But I also ask: what of the potential bobcats? The snakes? The devil's
cane that catches your legs if, heaven forbid, you wear shorts

while hiking? Better the shorts, however, than golden hair, a bright
red cape, or traveling with a brother who will also take

the tempting candy; who will keep walking
into the oven because he will always go the farthest.

FOR THE GIRLS IN THE COFFEEHOUSE
for JBB

Was I ever that at ease
with girls? Able to sit
with hips and shoulders,
heat and jean and flannel?
Or was I always
a bit sure I was other
with my last winter's jeans
in spring, my home cut hair?
Or is it not even about girls,
but more how I never
wanted to be boy
crazy; how I say, even now
as an adult, "He's a hugger
so sit down." When did it take
too much time out of my day
to engage in an embrace?
Maybe I've always
been an Alice, never able
to decide whether to eat
or drink the one that says
enjoy over the one that says
or not.

G: THE GIRL SAYS
after James Autio

Of course, she's bent
over. That's how
you reach the cord,
swinging from a thoracic

vertebrae. Pull it.
G: The Girl Says
Yes, most of the time
or *Certainly* or *Awesome*

or another of a handful
of positive words.
There is only a 13%
chance that she'll

say *No*. Or *Stop*. Or
Maybe which may
as well be a *Yes*
that just means

*Not right now, but I'll
give in later when I
feel guilty at standing
upright for anything.*

ZOMBIE GIRL EXPLAINS WHY SHE DOESN'T DATE

Maybe I could, but I just don't feel a need for fumbling in backseats, furtive phone calls, first this, first that. And with who? Imagine if I thought I might be queer—and a zombie. Although my mother would love it. I think she wishes she wanted women in that way. But I don't really want either sex in any way. Can you be human and asexual like say a seahorse? They are, right? I can't look it up. There is no way I'm typing *sex* into any computer attached to my name. Then the talks will start again. Mom will push my hair back behind my ears and rub each of my fingers between her index finger and thumb like she is cataloging them. One little piggy. Her little piggy. White as snow. How white. Virgin white. White as a keyboard. Save document. Control Alt Delete. Lock computer.

GAIJIN
Japanese word meaning foreigner, outside person

Forever, it seems, I have been suspicious
of girls; of the way they love

to have their nails painted; of their chatter
over the roar of hair dryers

or the GPS. Girls are always in motion.
Instead of sitting, they

pose on the edge of couches with legs
caved into each other.

They whisper. They jump rope to rhymes.
They must visit the bathroom

at least in pairs. I wonder if I just have
less estrogen, a failed

uterus, a want of pants and the thrust
of a car at sixty on a bumpy road.

Girls as cliché, holding hands until they
long for masculine fingers.

In Japan, the girls hide their smiles
behind their hands

and I understand this cultural quirk.
The consistency of it

makes me unafraid to watch them;
to picture myself in white makeup.

THE GIRL

The Girl with the curly blonde hair had been to Africa. *With my mom though,* she said. Her mother, an award-winning high school history teacher, had won the trip. I'd had her mom, the teacher, for two classes. I understood The Girl. *I think being choked by a beautiful man would be a nice way to go,* she said. The Girl had not mentioned sex but it was implied like John Donne's little deaths. "Oh! the places" The Girl was willing to go: to dyeing her hair an obvious red, to learning to drive a stick so she could have an open-door jeep at 16, to a college as far away in the state as was geographically possible. The Girl said, *with the right person it doesn't even hurt,* in answer to a question I never heard.

GIVE ME A G!
for Melanie

Since no one has created you, I will,
even though I cannot draw a circle
that doesn't look like a pear; I must
paint you with words whether or not

it sounds cliché you will fly, Geek
Girl. Your cape, to me, is green. You
wear stylish, boxy black frames
even though Superman offered you

laser eye surgery. You wear a "G"
on your chest, written in an Arial font.
You read minds, wear sweat pants
because it is cold inside clouds.

In your free time, you write it all down.
Your typing sounds like the last hurried
seconds of microwaving popcorn
before you know the bag is beginning

to burn. Your never ruin your snacks.
You smell the moment when the pop
is perfect. Like how your skin is perfect,
because your second secret power is

moisturizing. When you are trying
to hide the Geek Girl, you wear skirts
and contacts that change your eyes
from brown to Elizabeth Taylor purple.

You play dumb.

HALF-PINT

I used to assume that everyone
wanted to be Laura because I
wanted to be Laura.

Her Papa's Half-Pint, brown hair—
like mine—in braided pigtails.
But I've met Mary and Carrie

wannabes, even a few Nellies
who were so perpetually
optimistic that deep down

Nellie was a nice person—
just misunderstood. Or
maybe it was the money.

Or that even when caught, Nellie
still got away with being mean.
And there is that age—

when we just want to flail
out into ugliness. There was
even one girl I've met

who wanted to be
Albert even after I explained
he was a TV fabrication.

As if, she said, any of them
were anything close
to reality. As if

I could ever be
Daddy's little girl.

HIDDEN TREASURE

From a yard sale I bought a jewelry box of pressed orangey wood
which had three small drawers on the right side and one long
plastic door on the left
stenciled with a white oval.

On the left I hung my necklaces.
In the top two drawers I stowed rings
and charms. But the bottom drawer was shorter.
Behind it I hid my meager money. The bills
earned from mowing a lawn, watching
a child, or skipping lunch
at school.

But he found it there and in my shoe and somehow,
even in the last place I thought a father would go—
an underwear drawer.

HOARDERS

When we visit, you point out things you want us to have
after you die. You've been doing this since before
you turned fifty. The items you mention are "antiques"
or collectibles, knick knacks and the rare actual

heirloom item like the family Bible. I don't really
want any of it, although I am fond of those two
fat bear cubs which are made out of some swirly,
opaque glass. The ones in the locked cabinet

behind the table in the kitchen. The only locked
cabinet among the many that line the graying walls
of every room including the bathrooms. You never
mention the smaller items—the photographs, the

handmade ornaments, the things that we have given you.
Do they automatically revert back to the giver
after you die? What would I do with the stainless steel
paper clip holder I gave you while you were still working?

I keep paper clips in a box, an orange and black
lacquered one that was given to me as a gift
by a girl whose last name I don't even recall. When I
die, who will return it to Rebecca Something?

IT'S 4 AM WHEN I FINALLY GET IT

4 AM and I have to get up.
My hungover heels ache
from yesterday's walk/jog
as I try to stand.

In the bathroom I hover,
unsure why I don't turn on the light.
The door is closed. The slight crack
of incandescence shouldn't wake anyone,

but I'm already in position. I can't
imagine being a man, standing up
to urinate in the dark. I'm not
drunk but this half-awake stumbling

is as close as I get to understanding
inebriation. It would be so simple,
now seated, to close my eyes,
to nod off like he had when we found him.

DISCARDED

Under the chair to my right, still wrapped in white
plastic and stamped with pink flowers,
lies a tampon, diagonal to a heel—
the hell of sharp, black boot.

Yesterday, I stepped
on a tampon. It was reclining,
like an albino slug on a grey
brick walkway. It slid out
from my sneaker, smudged
with red, piedmont mud.

When I see them,
I lean over,
almost touching them.

This morning the tampon
was hanging from a tree,
the plastic removed, the cardboard
applicator gone. It had rained and the white
tube of fiber had fleshed out
like an opaque hourglass.

HABIT FORMING

Becky was a scab picker,
her skin: white divots.

On the bus no one sat with her,
saying "lice ridden" "rat bitten"

"so poor she shares a bed
with her brother" which was

somehow such a bad thing.
I'd sit in the back of the bus

where the older kids played
Truth or Dare; where, behind

raised jackets, I touched
a boy's pale penis; where

whispers started about what
you would do for a quarter—

voices that began to say
chew your hair, your nails,

the inside skin of your lip.

(HOW) THIN THE FINGERS

1

We held hands in church:
church, steeple, inside people.

2

What I thought, maybe,
was that I could be Marie Curie:

wife, mother, researcher,
teacher, scientist, winner.

3

I studied the Greeks, how
they used a Phoenician
alphabet full of consonants
(or CNSNNTS) thanks
to Cadmus, whose sister
Europa was abducted
by Zeus. But that's
an old story: Zeus and his
desires. I needed a fresh
set of letters, a new narrative.

4

Squeeze – Calcium – Milk or Sugar – Louis Pasteur –
Cheese – Coagulation – Merger of bits into bone – It all
decays – Rickets – Teeth – Vitamin D – Seaweed – Sesame
Seeds – Open – Wound – Fat Content – Osteoporosis –
Stress – Squeeze – Squeeze

5

It seems natural,
gravity, but explain
how it works.

It's like trying
to paraphrase God
or any other feat

of Biology. It's
like listening
to that five pound

squishy homunculus
in your skull,
that blathering

ball of neurons
who can't often tell
instinct from intuition.

(How) Frail the atoms.
(How) Thin the fingers
pressed against temples;

against the pain
of thinking, thinking
of all . . . of this.

(How) See through
the palms crossed
over a God-sized

hole in your heart.

I WANT TO BE A BOY

If I was a boy
I'd fall for you

and your southern
lisp   your

stereotypical limp-
wristed yet toned

arms And Oh
heavens those

green eyes like
ripe avocado

your pink palms
of bitten

strawberry
could be

on my hip   If
I was a boy I'd

be yang for your
yang because

opposites
don't always

attract Sometimes
like calls to like

and they
recognize

the shape the
smell the

feel of
perfect

apples all
from the same tree.

IRIS

Gull – heron – who is who –
the owl whose head moves
unnatural to our necks'
90 degrees – on lookout –
on Hatteras – hermit crab –
horseshoe – inland
cottonmouth – I learned
the word bestiary – robin –
bluebird - cardinal on my
perpendicular arm – the strong
brown boy who holds
my wrists and I
windmill – rainbowed

(IN)COMPLETE PATTERN

We were so interwoven that our classmates called us girlfriends, twisting the word away from its initial cotton of friendship into the silk of sex. Not that we were afraid of women who love women, but we were angry at still being unseen-unrealized-misinterpreted-mispronounced as we tried to 9 block a quilt together from our dissimilar lives; a blanket that could then be wrapped, folded, rolled into the thinnest of ropes that could withstand mean girls, mutual crushes, and competitive GPAs. I wanted the warp to last because I am not good at sisterhood. You welcome the feminine: wear it like a shawl against your simple, yet chic frame while I lumber without lipstick, laughing too loud. I see differences so easily. I call them out. You said once I was fickle, a complainer. I balked, but I did always see the missed stitches in everyone else's hem. If you saw those mistakes, you rarely commented. You'd rather repair while I choose to discard. Where I doubt; you know. You *are*; I am still trying to *be*.

THE POWER IS OUT

in Just- / spring when the world is mud- /
luscious the little lame balloonman / whistles

- ee cummings "in Just"

1

with a turn
I am dancing
with my palm
pressed to my hip
I am
my own partner

2

in the dark   even
when I leave
my eyes open
they shape
the night
into something
near recognition

3

my ears   prick
sound
I smell spring
in light fixtures
now balloon-like
just   out   of   reach
Dark
          and
far
and
wee

FAR AND WEE

I

Breathing on trees was my hobby. I'd sit on the browned pine needles, leaning my head against the bark, and I'd suck in as much air as I could through my nose then let it go with my chin pointed up to the branches. I'd pretend I was blowing up a balloon as I willed my carbon to keep the trees growing up and out.

II

I was never good at making balloons. Impatience perhaps? The first long breaths are almost futile. The balloon just spurts the air back at you, but if you keep pushing past that the plastic will eventually give and expand from the center rounding out.

III

Mom was the best at tying the ends of balloons, but my brother would do in a pinch. Like when we were waiting in the car once and to entertain us, my brother blew up a balloon for each of us. My sister was in the front seat, bouncing her balloon back and forth against the windshield, but I had taken a dare from my brother. I put the balloon under my shirt to pretend I was pregnant. I was rubbing my new rotund belly, saying, "Feel it kick!" When it popped, shrinking against the skin of my stomach, it pulled the flesh up and in.

LEADING THE SHOW

First grade – Ringling Bros. – three rings – high in the rafters –
a dollar for a Chinese yo-yo or cotton candy – it's like eating
air my friend says so I go for the toy – I whip it in front of me
– over my classmates heads thinking of leading the show –
come one – come all – see the bearded lady – the lobster boy –
the beautiful shapes of what is possible – but they aren't in
the show, those side show "freaks" – this circus is all tired
looking horses – trapeze with a net – motorcycles round and
round in a cage – but with my yo-yo I can point to a ring and
my friend's eyes will follow – I lead her to the clowns – to the
elephant trying to balance on a ball – back to the clowns –
back to the clowns.

LEFTOVERS

My dolls wore washcloths for dresses and rubber band belts.
They ate their unicorn cakes from washed-out TV dinner
trays. They had tea cups. A princess set, although the saucers
were missing. I took to placing the cups atop almost unused
spools of thread. The colors of the thread determined the taste
of the drink. Red for pomegranate, white for meringue, black
for tea which only the stuffed bears wanted, as they were
British. Sometimes I would cut out ads for newspaper pork
chops so we could have a main course. Next to me, my
German Shepherd would sit, a sphinx, waiting for bones.

LITERATURE OF MATH

Everyday math is one plus two. Commercial math. How to calculate a 20% tip is easier than 15. (I'm a good tipper.) Grocery store math. Would you like paper or plastic math? Then math turns to theory. $E = mc^2$. Colossal math. Math that adds dimensions and parallel worlds. Numbers that would be too big and fat to fit on a page. Think of pi. Numbers that go beyond binary, that stretch into narrative.

LAMB IN THREE PARTS

1

Mary had one
but it wasn't little,
small, tiny, micro-sized;
it was more like
an elephant, a mammoth even;
wooly and perhaps mean spirited,
angry, edgy, hip.

2

Mary spells her name
with an i now, chooses
lambkin555 for her screen name,
photoshops her 4-H project
until it is puppy-sized. She is
creating her legend; fleecing
her way up Reddit, Digg,
Stumbleupon until a dinosaur
in a tutu or a plane
with teeth are surreal enough
for social bookmarking success.

3

Mari (Mary)'s lamb grows
again but it never goes viral;
it doesn't go zombie, but
with Mary (Mari) it is sure
to go—go.

LINGUISTICS

Scared of math for decades,
I try to recite a few digits
of pi, admitting everything
comes back to numbers:

the three strokes to make
an upper case A, its three
points of connectivity
and the implied triangle.

We like to see solidity
in a letter even though
the sound of each vowel
rings differently from each

voice; yet a number
is always a constant. This
2 is the same 2 anywhere—
at least in our universe—

which is all, after all, we
are able to comprehend
because we want a point
that stays even as we

marvel at the hundreds
of folds in an aged
face of indeterminate
years or the complex

origami designed now
on computers; or

the theory that everything
is as flexible as string. Yet,

and still it comes back
to yet, and the questions
forever created
by the unconnected

hook and eye
of punctuation.

AN EXTRAPOLATION OF THE MOVIE *LABYRINTH* IN THREE PARTS

1

It was all about David Bowie's
crotch. At a sleepover, we wondered
whether or not the filmmakers
had been aware of the singer's 3D
like bulge. Dance Baby Dance.

2

It's a story to get lost in
about a place to get lost in, one
with goblins or trolls on every
upside down staircase like an Escher
painting or the mix-upped hallways
of the Winchester Mystery House
with its door to nowhere.

3

When you put yourself
into the narrative you prepare.
Before you agree to enter, you
procure a ball of thread made
from one of Iman's wigs that,
when unraveled, makes you forget
whether you want to leave or stay
because all you need is to lie down
on her hair's plush piles where you
can dream of sharp corners and turns
that flesh out into cylinders, then circles,
or cartoon dots that wormhole
you anywhere because they contain each
and every point of all abandoned
and unsolved puzzles which
are now yours to name.

NOT A SPOILER

There was no way I could avoid it.
And, no, I'm not one to give in
to peer pressure. But I had to see
what all the hype was about.

I cringed as I handed over
my debit card and I didn't
turn down the plastic bag
like I normally would. I didn't

want to be seen carrying a copy
of *Twilight*. It was a few
more weeks until I picked up
the fat paperback and started

reading. I was quickly annoyed
by sentence structure and flat
characterization. But I had
to finish. I wanted to know

what would happen. The book
was all plot without substance
like the way jell-o feels on your
tongue. I knew I wouldn't be

able to stomach actually buying
and reading the rest of the series
when I had so many other
wonderful books to choose from,

so I went online and found
plot summaries. I won't write
a spoiler, but I'm quite glad
I stopped with the first one.

WHEN PRE-TEENS WATCH SCARY MOVIES

We found you in the closet where you'd formed a womb
from two sleeping bags. You slept between them—
not inside—choosing the cool slick of nylon

over thermal cotton. We shouldn't have let you watch *It*.
Good thing we hadn't shown you *Poltergeist*
because the closet wouldn't have been any safer

than the bed we shared, underneath which I'd see
the red, glowing eyes from *Something Evil*.
How I wish we'd had a bed skirt.

Do you still pull aside the shower curtain
when you enter a bathroom even though
Psycho was outside the shower when he killed?

I'm not a psychiatrist but I made your hiding place
a womb instead of a sarcophagus even though
that is what I first thought of. Then of a rabbit hole.

VISIONS OF THE MONSTER

1

This is my Hulk paintbrush:
green bristles and purple shaft.
With him I work it out
because you wouldn't like me
when I'm angry and without
my tool, my . . . it isn't a weapon
although it is an instrument to inflict
—not just harm—but damage
and sometimes (think of tilling
up soil for a garden) there has to be
destruction first.

2

Inside a plain red box
a Hulk action figure
waits on white tissue paper.
Arms above his head
ready to SMASH. His legs
rotate with internal
rubber bands. My grandfather's
gift to me. Far better
than the blonde doll
as tall as me that—look—grandma says—
can walk if you move its arms
while you walk backwards.

3

Of a certain generation
we all remember the show,
the theme music, Bruce Banner,
mild-mannered until . . .
and that's when your parents
would call you because you
only wanted to see
the change, to watch
the strong man
taking down the bad guy.

NOT THE SUNDAY FAMILY MOVIE NIGHT

See the red trampoline tongue
Shaggy DA
How many comedies
are made
out of unexpected
transformations?
Except
when there is a pink
thong on a teen boy
who knows he is a girl
who just has too much of
. . . something
Too absent of . . .
other
He/she twirls knowing
they will be a lawyer:
Special Victims Unit
or a Vet
for little cats
homely dogs
The unclear sex
of the un-prodded rabbit

THE MUMMY

She planned on being a cowboy
for Halloween. Not a cowgirl.
Not the girl with a lasso

and a skirt but the boy with a pistol
and chaps; both with hats,
spurs, and fringe.

Instead she is ringing door after door
wrapped in loose scraps of sheets,
explaining she is a mummy.

She can't, however, tell
how her costume
is a punishment

because she was caught
with an ace bandage
wound tightly;

how she used it to speak
down her breasts
which were so

talkative against her undershirts.
You just don't do that
her mother said.

You just don't.

MUFF

On certain fowl, they are the feathers clustered on each side of the head. Perhaps from the dutch *mof* (mitten).

As clothing—a tunnel for the hands. See *Little House on the Prairie.* From Middle French *moufle.*

In sports it is to miss a catch, to bungle. From Medieval Latin: *muffula* (a fur-lined glove).

When used as slang: the covering hair or the internal channel.

Think decoration, think warmer, think hot potato, think clever euphemism that is a double entendre which boasts a double-edged sword.

If seen in a dream then girls you have good luck looming. But boys? Be warned of this image. For you it means your girl has found that good fortune elsewhere, and you'll soon be cold, not cool, ice-edged.

MY NERD BOY

You walk on your heels as if they are bananas.
You have a bad complexion: red and mountainous.
But you are brave enough to jump from trees,
to climb without monkey arms. You drop to me,
calling me: dream. You speak of places
where moisture begins; where it starts to pool.
You speak with your tongue against
my thigh with its y-shaped vein.

OXYGEN IS OBVIOUS

like Britney Spears
like how I knew one day
she'd shave
(insert body part here)
because she's been
straddling the line
between Mouseketeer
and toxic exotic
dancer since . . . . Well
if paparazzi found
her ultrasound photos
they'd see Britney pushing
her best bits forward
even in the womb
abhorring the tight
umbilical cord
and how closed
it is the fetal form.

OR

you can sit on the shore,
he said, when I couldn't
explain why pulling
the oar towards me
made the boat go forward.
It just works, I said.
A ripple of moisture
formed along the bottom
of my eye where I'd
attempted to apply
eyeliner for the first time.
He'd never before
offered to take me fishing.
I didn't have the scientific
words for the meditative
motion of rowing, but I
was a stronger swimmer,
a good rower. For once,
I had the physical covered.
I went back inside
the house noting that words
could fail me.

ODE TO THE PERPETUAL LOSER

Why not the anvil?
Its cartoon
effectiveness free-
falls on the hapless
anti-hero, the one
I know because I too
cannot catch; do not
quite fit; will not keep
up without fret and bushed
out brows. If not
the anvil, piano, barrel
of bricks, then
what music? How to harness
the clang of cacophony,
the awful cheers
of the audience
who needs to laugh.

THINGS THAT ARE OUT TO GET YOU

Orcs ogres ordained ministers
Pterodactyls psoriasis Pennywise the Clown
Quarks family quilts questions
Reviews of your books
Salmonella salamanders Stockholm Syndrome
Tendonitis torsion time travel
Unicorns on unicycles
Vulcans volcanoes vapid vactioneers
White lies whistles woe-be-goneness
X marks your spot
Yesterday
Zombies zebras
Altruism
Babies bigots ballroom dancing
Curves clones colonics
Demons drag queens Dunkin Donuts
Education escalators elephantitis
Flatulence fungus
Garbage grit grime
Hands handouts
Ice-picks inspiration
Judge jury
Kleptomaniacs kisses
Melons melon ballers melanoma
Nepotism naugahyde Fig Newton calories

-OLOGY

1. Physical Science

Chewing wintergreen Lifesavers burns my gums, but I gnash
my teeth in front of the mirror to watch sparks sprout—
Triboluminescence.

2. Biology

At my desk, I draw a thread through the epidermis on the tips
of my fingers and palm, lacing my hand into a white spider
web that hangs from a branch—my arm.

3. Sociology

A small blonde girl sits on the lap of a large blond boy. She
gulps in air while he clasps his hand into a knot that he pulls
into her body. She flops. Her back rests against his chest, her
head a humid leaf—Truth or Dare.

4. Mythology

We pile leaves—copper, yellow, and red. I light a match. She
takes it as the flame climbs and tosses it onto the heap where
holes spread across the leaves as they fold into themselves.
Squatting, I poke the growing ash with a stick. I think of
Prometheus and how—for this—I'd give up my liver for a
while.

PHYSICAL SCIENCE

When my stepfather returned from his long haul to Florida,
he handed us fireworks from South Carolina.

I was the lighter. You were the watcher.

I pulled the match against the box. You watched
as the fire bit the air and crawled up the fuse.

In the backyard, I tossed the firecrackers
onto the concrete slab where they jumped like flying fish.

The last one went off in my hand.

My hand went numb; my fingertips un-whorled.
Your voice sounded like the ocean held inside a shell

against my ear.

From my hair, I pulled charcoal paper shaped
like tiny curlers. You

laughed at how only my left cheek turned red.

I wanted to cry,
but I stuck my tongue out at you

as I rubbed my fingertips together
pushing out the numbness.

THE PALE TUMBLE

Of course Heath (the one I can't call Ennis)
was in the white hat. Of course he was the one
who tried to play it straightest: blond, wife,
children while Jake/Jack is dark, black-hatted,
the one who makes the first drunken move.

He also tries marriage, and (from what I hear)
that's as exciting as it gets. Even the gay men
I know said the sex scene was awkward,
that it was the only reason they saw the movie—
that they waited for it to come out on DVD

if they were only one foot, one hand, a belt
buckle out of the closet. Even the author
of the original short story (which I read, which
felt as long as a desert) is tired, especially
of the fan fiction she receives. Can you imagine?

People fixing your story with details of hand
placement; of the men in nothing but hats
and the pale tumble of bodies where skin
matches the color of sand; of dusk, marked with
dark chips of what might be stone, follicle;

of the just almost out of frame black brim.

PERPETUAL MOTION

As I pick at the change
from my cupholder,

I flip over one quarter
that seems slim.

1970. Older than me.
There is a divot

over the 9 and the 7.
I stroke

at Washington's
braid and wonder

if maybe a young groom
had rubbed

this quarter while he
waited for his bride.

I can see the church, small,
but not without

the same sound of those colossal
cathedrals like the Sacre

Coeur where the stairs to the tower
have gone concave

down the center of each step.
When I was there

I tried to walk as close to the wall
as possible, as if

my little feet in my one visit
could somehow

work away a noticeable
bit of stone.

POLAROID

You sit on the edge
of the red recliner.
We are both
dressed in white
for bedtime. I'm on
my back, my legs
at a 90 degree angle.
You are holding
my feet, eating
my feet, like
the tickle monster
would do if he
gave up on
gitchy gitchy goo.
I'm a little
demon, my hair
never succumbing
to the exorcism
of a comb. My
mouth a lower
lipped pout
of why-why-why?
We, a pair
of cannibals
because I eat
your time
which is as rare
as the pictures of us
together. How to,
therefore, compare
a look of joy versus
terror? We mirror.

POWER

1.

With our fists filled with lettuce,
we feed the goats, our wrists
suspended over the wire fence.

My brother says, "Wood will complete
the circuit; metal will keep you grounded."
I have heard of lightning rods protecting homes

during storms, and I know you shouldn't
shelter under trees during thunder
so I believe my brother. I pick up an old

bicycle handlebar and approach the fence.
The electricity knocks me back. My
brother laughs and runs in circles.

I get up, tingling, and walk towards
the wire again.

2.

For Christmas, I receive
a Simon Says. I take the battery
from the TV remote and watch

as the game lights up. Red. Red Yellow.
Red Yellow Yellow. My sister
whines because I keep winning.

I say we can play Truth or Dare
instead, knowing she'll always
take a dare. I pull the battery

back out, dare her to lick it.
She yips with the 9 volt in her hand.
She yanks it away from her wet tongue

that arches out of her mouth. I grab
the battery from her so I can take a turn.

(PARENT)HETICAL

It's the breaking of the f(our)th wall, a chip in the mortar of expected dialogue. It says, *Welcome*. It's dramatic irony as it was traditionally de(fine)ed and not just slang, not just an everyday word like Mom or Dad or Stepmother or dead or unav(ail)able or tir(ing). It's a side track for the audience, an unanticipated trip into the author as (parent)al figure (who) leads on with her plot, h(is) character, (an)d any other *it* that is wrapped up in the person, place, thing, or (idea) of a noun.

THE CHRISTMAS PAGEANT

Every year: the same show.
The sixth graders (our seniors)
as Santa and reindeer.

The first graders portrayed
"The Night Before Christmas."
I was the littlest stocking.

In my pink footie pajamas, I stood
last in line by height next to the red
and white painted cardboard mantle.

I was the smallest first grader
as would be my sister two years later
and my other sister five years after that.

We probably wore the same PJs
just as there are photos of us
each wearing the same

dresses in kindergarten.
We each were pegged
in third grade to be the littlest

angel. We should have taken home
the thin white robe and tinsel-
covered weak and bending wings

because those roles stayed in our family.
We had a genetic pre-disposition
for the bit parts.

PETS

What do little Japanese girls
dream of while their American
counterparts pet stuffed
unicorns? Do those Asian
pre-teens buy poseable
My Little Ponies as plastic
pet replacements or are those
girls more enthralled by
pandas, tiny chittering
monkeys, or sleek
untouchable koi? On which
creatures do they practice?

QUEST

Of course I find myself in the library,
the card catalog, a well-organized friend.

It's a Wednesday; I pick a letter;
flip the tactile cards; then hunt

a heft of a book with an obvious
center that takes me

to a goateed horse with a severe horn
leaning against a thin tree inside a small

circular fence. A cage. Like a Celtic
ring. He, I think he's a he,

is calm but tail alert.
He's caught but not

trapped. If he unfurled
those beautiful legs

he could easily exit the enclosure.
I wonder where

I picked up the word
Celtic? I don't want

to leave him but I must go
to the dictionary or

the encyclopedia, anything
in the reference

room where beginnings
have beginnings

and where I can touch
the cold slip of microfiche.

RANDOM THINGS I LOVED AS A CHILD
before anyone told me better

- a metal Kiss lunch box
- a black baby doll
- a Darth Vader helmet necklace
- a blue jeans purse (acid washed)
- a Superman plane with activated fists
- bunk bed hammocks
- stuffed animal Olympics
- Hardy Boys novels
- Hawaiian shirts
- Bologna with the red strip meticulously pulled
  while watching *Shazam!* or *Tom and Jerry*
  or *Little House on the Prairie*

(RE) IMAGINING
after Jack Gilbert

It's a shame that memory only works in (re)verse; that music
must be made for what never happened because memoir is
never a photograph but more a poem, a collage of the food
fight that was only one can tossed against a wall and not the
f(re)nzy of ketchup coated F(re)nch fries against the sliding
glass doors that is instead written because we all want the
inte(re)sting story—the d(re)am time of (re)imagining; the
chance to make new words without centers like fnzy,
fnch, inte, sting, dam.

SISTER OF THE (MAP) MAKER

My brother was in charge of the map.
He always needed an activity.
The only child backseat driver I ever knew.

He plotted paths of hurricanes,
was on the Quiz Bowl team,
read novels of alternate histories.

I thought I was the sole survivor
of our tumultuous household,
but his coping mechanisms

were just different. In the van,
while I waved to truck drivers,
he wore X-ray goggles,

trying to see beyond the yellowing
stalks of corn towards some zenith
above and most importantly

beyond where we currently were.
I couldn't see further than college.
That was always my dream.

He envisioned careers: engineering,
meteorology, fine robotic design.
I got that degree. He got a job—

had lots of jobs, a family.
I got stuck with a piece of paper,
and a job that didn't match up.

He knew how to take apart and put together
radios, toasters, lego towers of ships ready for liftoff.

SCIENTIFIC METHOD

I wanted dimples like my Daddy. Sitting in front of the TV, I'd push my index fingers into the fleshiest parts of my cheeks. I waited for the fat to give—to divot like the world would pivot when I would spin across the room, falling down to watch the earth in its natural rotation.

SOUNDTRACK

Maybe your first slow dance
was to "Stairway to Heaven"
or perhaps "Thriller" was
not only your favorite song
that encompasses all of third grade,
but it was also playing
on an oldies station when you picked
your daughter up from her first group
movie date. I could play along.
How about "Living on a Prayer" and how
I grew my hair long. How I dreamed
of rising up to be a waitress just working
for love. How I was too young to get
the cheekiness of the album title
"Slippery When Wet," but how
I was still close enough to understanding
as I examined the CD insert containing
photos of the band. How my face
flushed as I pondered the mystery
of chest hair and tight leather pants.

TEEN GEEK

Who did you hang
on your wall? Were you
all about Tom Cruise or
one of the Corey's? I
was a geek lover, wanting
my dream date to be
Lloyd Dobler from
Say Anything or
Farmer Ted from
Sixteen Candles
and I mean
the characters because
I had no illusions
of ever meeting
John Cusack or
Anthony Michael Hall
even if every girl I knew
who had been to Myrtle Beach
claimed to have seen
someone famous there.
Even if I went there, I'm sure
the only guy who would follow
me would be wearing high
waters or sporting taped up
thick framed glasses. Real
geeks weren't as interesting,
real dorks were everywhere.
I wanted my nerds
with a hint of cute,
the kind of everyday boy
that could be a prince
if you kissed him.

TO THE TINY COWBOY

boot swaying from the ball
hitch of a clay-streaked
SUV: I hope you

are well. Brown, silver
spurred, star
applique, you

are better than a set
of truck nuts,
although fake

testicles
next to
a tailpipe

makes sense
unlike you . . .
one of a usually

assumed pair
because we are
bipedal. They'd never

hang just one
truck nut, uneven
sack which makes

me think
you are a cowgirl,
riding your first steer.

THE TOYS OF MY CHILDHOOD

are back. Stop in any
Spencer's or Hot Topic
and you can pick up
a My Little Pony or
a new and improved
light saber. But the one
I want is a plush Super
Grover Doll. Can't you
just see Grover Kent
changing in a phone booth
because somewhere a child
is in distress? This one needs
convincing that haircuts
don't hurt. That one
doesn't understand
how to take the bus.
While Super Grover
flaps his cape and presents
a confused smile, the kids
always figure out
what to do on their own.
I want the doll, until I see
the $29.99 price tag
and figure—Wubba Wubba—
memory is cheaper.

THEY SAY *LET IT GO*

The blonde girl is spinning
like a sufi, like a dreidel, like
her twin from the subway.
The motion fans their hair
as they turn. One inside a church
the other holds a pole. Their eyes closed.

Yeah. You gotta let go.

Lita, the mother calls.
"Leda," someone sighs.
One named for a rock star.
The other raped by a swan.
And now one of the girls
is lost to crowds or bad
decisions or mythology or
is a "body laid in that white rush."

Yeah, you gotta let go.

And, if there was an answer
for why I see a girl in glee,
whirling against gravity,
and think violence
I would put it here
to get it out of my mind.

Yeah, you, gotta let go.

ZOMBIE GIRL TRIES SITTING
AT THE BACK OF THE BUS

For some reason, that day, she decided to play
Truth or Dare. She dared.

She leaned over to kiss the blondish boy
and she did encounter

soft like she thought she would, but there wasn't
any movement as she expected.

She opened her eyes onto her first real penis.
The other kids had

propped the boy against the back of the seat
so the zombie girl would be properly

aimed at his crotch. Did she think of crying?
Of throwing up?

What she did was crawl under the seat, swerving
to her right to reach the aisle

before she stood up and walked, without looking back,
to her normal seat at the front of the bus.

UNMASKED

What if all our heroes took off their masks?
What would you think if they had black
roots beneath their bleached blonde hair
or if they had freckles across their pointed

or dimpled chins? And what if you kept
looking and removed the cape, saw the stubs
of wings that never formed or the sharp
edges leftover after the shaving down,

necessary for the hero to fit better into
an invisible plane? Then, what if you kept going
and further in there were corsets to pull, tights
to strip off, platform boots to unzip, even skin

to unhinge? Would you want to check for kidneys
ready to be punched? Would you lay on the adjoining
table to compare your proportions? What would you do
if you found you had the same length of bone?

ZOMBIE GIRL SKIPS VALENTINE'S DAY

It is better this way,
her absence. I hate

that I was relieved
when the note came

from the office but now,
well, the other

students can just give out
their valentines. I

won't have to come up
with contingency plans

for her. I mean, what if
she had been given

none? What if she had tried
to hand out cards

and the other kids
threw them away?

What would she
have brought anyway?

Handmade paper hearts
painted black?

THE STUDY OF

I

Easing to the kitchen linoleum
I spread my legs
into a V

The stretch in my thighs feels sharp
and sweet
like pink plans
when I was all
ankles and baby-fist-sized
breasts pressing against
the skin
thin of a ribbed tank top

"Ribbed for my pleasure"
you said
I thought
what a terrible line
but I fell
instead
for your video
game wisdom

"Only the dead
carry hand grenades"

II

When we met
we were
lit up
filled

with hormones
and starbursts
like hydrogen
seeking oxygen

We met
at the X
like a chromosome
which is
the true apple
inside of Eve
that need
                to know
                to touch

and I
needed
small talk
afterwards so I asked
                is prejudice born
in our DNA

You said I was too young for anguish
that I loved the overpowering smell
of the anecdote
the taste
of nostalgia

III

I was still child enough
to jump into
air
to be someone
for seconds
                winged

You had Frito Lay
breath
and a beehive
tattoo

I had a beautiful spine

You held a low well
          of loneliness
shaded a green
I thought I could walk on

I had a small tongue
that wanted something
to lick

You said you'd catch me
that
falling was flying
                    without wings

IV

I wanted to be
in one of your lyrics

"because tonight feels like Paris
all diesel and yeast"

I wanted to have strawberry gelato
I wanted to sit under the steel skirt
                    of the Eifel Tower
                    again

because I'd been there

and to New York

"the sound of which
                              is in between subways"
on empty platforms

and I'd known Fridays

"rolled off like spent pantyhose
stretched out with one long run
                        snagged on a car door"
washed out by chapped hands

because you had been there

V

I craved the study
of you
but I learned
quiet
and how
to ask fewer questions
knowing
there were no standardized tests
        for us

because we agreed
evolution was a myth
a complex hoax
of bones and sediment

of marrow
and soft shoulders

of bits that did not form

A WRITER'S BLOC DENIAL IN ONE MINUTE

There is too much poetry of
poetry, of
a poet's love
of words, lines of

prepositions, forms as games, rhymes,
prepositions
strained to fit like
last spring's best white

T-shirt; that once unfolded is
origami creased
and just a bit
cold and too tight.

WRITE MY LIFE STORY

is what you say
when I call to tell you
I was accepted
into graduate school.
I'm a poet, I reply.
You tell me I should
be a real estate broker.
I don't like sales, I say.
You ask me
if I remember the time
you read one of my poems.
You laughed, I say,
which you find hysterical.

THE LETTER W
for Mindy

We are given an alphabet at birth.
Our names are spelled for us; our
small syllables are encouraged
as we test our tongues

against the taste of words. Yet
there is always a day or year
when we need a new vocabulary
because genetics are not enough

to define who we are. We may
have been called Eleanor or Eli,
but we choose to grow our hair
long and decide to be known

as The-One-Who-Braids or
we obtain a tattoo, a shaping of
characters on the skin that we only
know through translation because we

are too old to have been taught phonetics
in school but too young to have studied
when classics were required.
In between we think of being

surreal and dabble in defining
every day in 140 characters or less
until one moment or month
requires we speak into only the white space.

WALKING DICTIONARY

My mother never treated anything like an emergency. Patient.
When my brother got off the school bus to fight another boy,
my mom took care of it at home with stabilization and an ice
pack. "He has fractured his clavicle," she said. Who around us
would say that? They'd say something more along the lines
of, "He's done broke his collarbone." Not as a stereotype but
as a fact of diction. She said everything different like that. She
explained to me once that I was getting a urinary tract
infection because I was touching my labia in the bath. I was
only six, but somehow I knew not to use that word at school.
Labia. Not bath. No one wanted to hear about your UTI even
in grade school. Mom had wanted to be a librarian. She could
type faster than anyone I knew, never went anywhere without
a book. For her, when I practice yoga, I try to learn the Indian
words for the moves: Tadasana, Savasana.

NOT A BIG BANG, A BIG MAC

If I tell you it is my wyrd
that I am fat—that the cookie
and the nachos (veggie chili,
hold the sour cream) were necessary
because of the 32 oz soda
before that and the fries dipped
in ranch dressing from a week ago
or the salad nested inside a wall
of garlic croutons from a birthday
a month in the past or how about
the year previous when I bought
my own chocolate fountain in case
I wasn't alone on New Year's
or memories of buffets all the way, way back
to puberty and parents with a taste
for starch (both solid and liquid) who
met because of another couple
who didn't want to party alone
like the first microscopic bits
who decided bonding would be better
than solitarily strutting in front
of the drive-through window
at the beginning of the universe.

I SAW A WOMAN I COULD NOT BE
after Louis CK

The woman waddled. She wasn't fat, but maybe she was full (and/or tired) of carrying around the load of her two x chromosomes. She didn't yield to anyone on the street despite her wonky walk. She zoomed through the crowd. At the intersection she almost stopped, but really all she did was slow down as if to tell the taxis (and overly large cars unmeant for city life) that she was going to cross the street. I decided to follow her. She entered a deli. She didn't have to order her food. She sat down and the gentleman behind the counter brought her a covered plate. This was the perfect timing of a regular customer. I felt like I joined her when I sat at an adjacent table. I kept my cell phone out so I'd look busy, but I was really watching her. She seemed to live so minutely, neatly, orderly. I wondered if I should purchase something, but no one questioned me. I wasn't a regular, but the restaurant was relatively quiet so I just sat. She took up her fork and tackled her potato salad at an unusual pace. She started out slow, but then seemed voracious, un-embarrassed by her appetite. She was so very vital, this woman I could not be.

RADIATING GIRL

She's been X-rayed
five ways to yesterday—yearned
for sleep only to zone out
when she was awake enough to act out
a battle from *Band of Brothers*
with her cousins. She couldn't
dare spend much time with them—dare
to damage her immune system as if egging
her cells to fight or fry. She couldn't
decide if it was better to give up
or to hunker down beneath yet another machine.
She insisted she was pain free
and not just for the jell-o reward.
She wanted to keep lines away—
lines of nurses with needles, lines lengthening
her mother's face. Her mother's mask
no longer new. It needed
plastic surgery—an aggressive overhaul
to turn that frown upside down.
She could say that quietly
so her mother could render it mute
if she wanted or her mother could suck on it
like a too-old toddler still needing the teat.
She could hardly remember uniform, un-hospitalized days.
She was no longer upset by the other gurney veterans.
She smiled at the well-wishers who secretly thought: not me;
not mine.

THE X CHROMOSOMES SPEAK

We are obsessed with gravity.
How it reshapes our bodies.
Yet, it is the weakest
of forces. Think how easy
it is to overcome when we
skip. Gravity might say, "I
may be thin but isn't it
relative? After all, I affect
everything, everywhere."
We acknowledge the points
that gravity makes
as we rub a balloon
against our hair to create
static electricity,
a stronger power. Gravity
interrupts to say, "Without me
you would not exist. There
would be no way for your large
shape to stay together." We want
to reassure gravity that we love
him (his neediness feels masculine),
but we can't help being drawn
away from him and towards
the minute nuclear forces
that attract and repel each other;
the small bits too tiny to be seen
and, therefore, so much more
intriguing because of their
minute mysteries.

HISTORY LESSON

If there is an OM at the center of the breath and if that breath is a microcosm of the world, then sound will shape a body from blown sand, like a woman curved as an hour glass. Her head is revisionist history. Her torso is of now, of touch, of taste. Her lower body is tomorrow's tomorrow which emerges as hardened sand: all tiny ears and toes. Or is she desire's receptacle whose wants invent a macrocosm that says *off with her head* in favor of a new religion, of the need for a preponderance of the Y chromosome. That Y, the eternal drawing of the male, with all three lower limbs connected as one unit walking toward need. Above them, the arms are always up ready to fight with matching double-edged swords. Yet he also starts as open as spread wings.

YOU ARE TOLD

You are on your best behavior.
You sit zazen like she does.
You are trying to like arugula.
You are the only man in the belly dancing class.
You always push the shopping cart
so she can walk ahead, determining
the route you'll take even though every aisle
will be visited except she won't follow
the lawn-mower like graph you'd choose.
You haven't had a beer in a month.
Instead it is wine with dinner
or maybe a juice and vodka cocktail
while the kids take their baths.
You lather, rinse, repeat
your daughter's hair, wear a soap bubble mustache.
You never leave the toilet seat up.
You only urinate sitting down.
No pee will splash up on the pristine
toilet which you quickly scrub
after each use. You've never rented a movie
without asking her. You've never asked for odd sexual
adventures. You are tame, you are told,
but no one understands how much you just want
to be here—with a family even though you had a vasectomy
within weeks of your daughter's birth. Your wife decided
Xavier and Abby, exactly two kids, would be enough.

YOU NEVER HIT

She was supposedly an alcoholic,
but I'd never seen her drink.
You never said she beat you,
but I could tell she could be cruel.

But I'd never seen her drink.
Instead, anger in how she cooked.
I could tell she could be cruel:
the mashing, the pepper, the cast iron.

Instead, anger in how she cooked.
I say you called the kettle black:
the mashing, the pepper, the cast iron
as you drank, wallowed, and still loved her.

I say you called the kettle black.
She was supposedly an alcoholic.
As you drank, wallowed, and still loved her.
You never said she beat you.

(UN)REAL BATTLE

Who would win:
zombies or unicorns?

Both pale and at their base—
animals. Yet

the unicorn
is anthropomorphized

into being more human
than the formerly human

zombie and neither
can truly vocalize.

They each have a weapon:
teeth versus horn;

rock, paper, scissors.
Paper can cover rock.

Rock can crush paper.
Teeth bites off horn.

Horn cracks tooth.
What it will come down to

is luck, which one
lunges at just the right moment.

ACKNOWLEDGMENTS

These poems, sometimes in different form, have appeared in the following journals, literary magazines, and anthologies. Appreciation to the editors.

"Amphibiogenesis in Two Voices" - *Handshake (an Eardrum Pop Production)*

"At 13" and "The Power Is Out" - *Scythe Literary Journal*

"Everyone Named Her Bright," "Field Trip," and "What I Thought After Fabio Was Hit in the Face by a Bird at Busch Gardens" - *Wild Goose Poetry Review*

"Little Borders" - *Assisi Online Journal*

"New Kid" - *National Gallery of Writing*

"The Boy Who'd Never Seen Snow" and "Random Things I Loved as a Child" - *The Dead Mule School of Southern Literature*

"Short Girl at the Theme Park" and "Soundtrack" - *Iodine Poetry Journal*

"What Would Buffy Do?," "An Extrapolation of the Movie *Labyrinth* in Three Parts," and "The Letter W" - *Diverse Voices Quarterly*

"Zombie Girl's Lament," "Learning to Count," "The Girl," and "I want to be a boy" - *Wilderness House Literary Review*

"Diagramming Sentences" - *CRATE Magazine*

"Drawn to Heroes" - *The Northville Review*

"Dragon" - *Barely South*

"The Egg Dream" - *The Main Street Rag*

"Forest" - *WEAVE*

"Function of *X*" - *Lily*

"For the Girls in the Coffeeshop" - *LitSnack*

"Zombie Girl Explains Why She Doesn't Date" - *Tipton Poetry Journal*

"Gaijin" - *Empowerment4Women*

"Hoarders" - *Broad River Review*

"Hidden Treasure" and "Habit Forming" - *Camroc Press Review*

"Far and Wee" - *blue fifth review*

"Leftovers" and "The toys of my childhood" - *Red Dirt Review*

"Literature of Math – *ken*again*

"Not a Spoiler" - *pig in a poke*

"Not the Sunday Family Night Movie" and "Zombie Girl Tries Sitting at the Back of the Bus" - *Young American Poets*

"The Mummy" - *The Meadowland Review*

"MUFF" - *Marks Lit Journal*

"Nerd Boy" - *Steel Toe Review*

"Things That Are Out to Get You" - *Eye Socket Journal*

"Ode to the Perpetual Loser" - *H.O.D. (Handful of Dust)*

"Perpetual Motion" - *Praxilla*

"Power" and "(Parent)hetical" - *Rose & Thorn*

"The Christmas Pageant" and "Teen Geek" - *vox poetica*

"A Writer's Bloc Denial in One Minute" - *UCity Review*

"(Re)Imaging" - *Specter Magazine*

"Scientific Method" - *Weave Magazine*

"Zombie Girl Skips Valentine's Day" - *Magnapoets*

"Write my life story" - *Testing the Waters*

"The X Chromosomes Speak" - *Poetry East*

"(un)real battle" - *Southern Women's Review*

GRATITUDE

First off, a hats off for those who read the manuscript in its varied forms: Jenny Beaver for the title (and other things), Jessica Varin, Addy McCullough, Melanie Faith (as if all you do is just read, my friend!), and Ellaraine Lockie (who also created the amazing cover art specifically for this project). A big thank you for Bryan Borland for taking a chance on this book. I'm glad to be a part of your pirate crew. I also have to give kudos to my wonderful larger group of friends who are family and family who are friends, especially my husband, Ken, without whom this wouldn't be possible—or worth it.

ABOUT THE POET

Jessie Carty's poetry, fiction, and non-fiction have appeared in publications such as *Iodine Poetry Journal, decomP*, and *Connotation Press. Morph* is Jessie's second full length poetry collection. Her first book, *Paper House* (Folded Word, 2010), won the Northern California Poetry Award. Jessie is also the author of four chapbooks: *At the A & P Meridiem* (Pudding House, 2009), *The Wait of Atom* (Folded Word, 2009), *Fat Girl* (Sibling Rivalry, 2011), and *An Amateur Marriage* (Finishing Line Press, 2012) which was a finalist for the Robert Watson Prize. Jessie works as a freelance editor, writer, and writing coach/teacher. She is also an adjunct instructor in the First-Year Writing Program at UNC-Charlotte. Jessie founded the literary magazine *Shape of a Box*, YouTube's first literary magazine, as well the online journal *Referential Magazine* which is still in production. Jessie received her MFA from Queens University of Charlotte. [jessiecarty.com]

ABOUT THE PRESS

Founded in 2010, Sibling Rivalry Press is an independent publishing house based in Alexander, Arkansas. Our mission is to publish work that disturbs and enraptures. We are proud to be the home to *Assaracus*, the world's only print journal of gay male poetry. Our titles have been honored by the American Library Association through inclusion on its annual "Over the Rainbow" list of recommended LGBT reading and by *Library Journal*, who named *Assaracus* as a best new magazine of 2011. While we champion our LGBTIQ authors and artists, we are an inclusive publishing house and welcome all authors, artists, and readers regardless of sexual orientation or identity. [siblingrivalrypress.com]

CPSIA information can be obtained at www.ICGtesting.com
Printed in the USA
LVOW10s1652150913

352507LV00002B/35/P